I0644308

Songs

LEVEL 6

/ee/
/e_e/

DECODABLES BY jump!

Teaching Tips

Orange Level 6

This book focuses on the phonemes **/ee/e_e/**.

Before Reading

- Discuss the title. Ask readers what they think the book will be about. Have them briefly explain why.
- Ask readers to name the missing letter for each word on page 3. What do they notice about the "e" sound in these words? Is the "e" a long or short vowel in each?

Read the Book

- Encourage readers to break down unfamiliar words into units of sound. Then, ask them to string the sounds together to create the words.
- Urge readers to point out when the focused phonics phonemes appear in the text.

After Reading

- Encourage children to reread the book independently or with a friend.
- Ask readers to name other words with /ee/ or /e_e/ phonemes. On a separate sheet of paper, have them write the words out.

5357 Penn Avenue South
Minneapolis, MN 55419
www.jumplibrary.com

Decodables by Jump! are published by Jump! Library.

Library of Congress Cataloging-in-Publication Data is available at www.loc.gov or upon request from the publisher.

ISBN: 979-8-88996-867-2 (hardcover)
ISBN: 979-8-88996-868-9 (paperback)
ISBN: 979-8-88996-869-6 (ebook)

Photo Credits
Images are courtesy of Shutterstock.com. With thanks to Getty Images, Thinkstock Photo and iStockphoto. Cover – poltu Shyamal. 2–3 – ungvar, elesi, Antlii, OlegRi. 4–5 – DmitryStock, StockImageFactory.com, VALUA VITALY. 6–7 – Ronald Sumners, strelka. 8–9 – Anton27, fizkes. 10–11 – Africa Studio, Monkey Business Images. 12–13 – Eleonora_os, Natalja Mizinova. 14–15 – AnnaStills, CGN089. 16 – Shutterstock.

Can you fill in the gaps?

concre_e

the_e park

dele_e

e_ening

There are lots of different songs. Songs can make us feel sadness or glee. What songs do you like?

You might not like all songs that you hear, but you do not need to. People do not agree on what the best song is. You are free to like what you like!

Some songs are serene and slow. You can sway along to these songs. Hearing these songs at night can help you sleep.

Serene means relaxing.

Some songs are not serene at all. An extreme song might have loud drums and screeching sounds in it.

Some songs get people tapping their feet to the beat. Songs with a fast beat are fun to dance to.

Do you tap along to the beat?

A show might have a song that plays a lot. This is a theme song. You might hear a theme song at the start or end of a show.

Singing is a talent. Some people are good singers, but they have to practice to get better.

Songs often have a theme. This is what the song is about.

The different sounds and themes in a song might make people think about different things.

Songs can be long or short. They can have electronic noises or noises from keys or strings.

An artist can spend weeks or even years on one song. They have to think of what they want to say in the song and what sort of beat to use.

An artist may need much longer than that to complete an album.

Point to the objects that have /ee/ in their name.

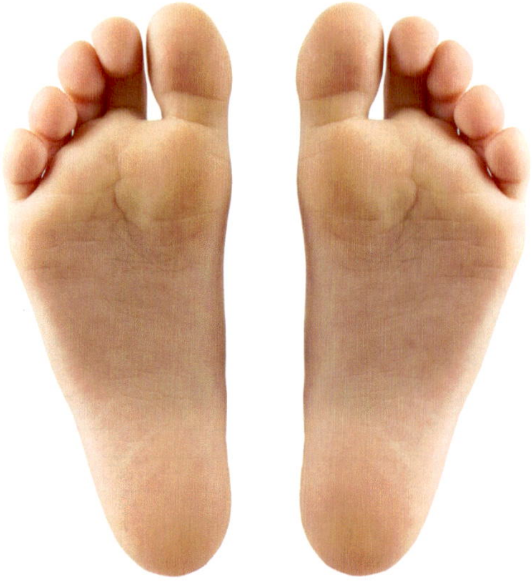